People look at you strange, say you changed. Like you worked that hard to stay the same. - Jay-z

.Coolgmack@gmail.com

Characters drawn by"Pcgraphiczz"
https://www.fiverr.com/pcgraphiczz

SUCKER
4
LOVE

By

Coolgmack

LOVE

Love is not just a four-letter word it's an action
It's the satisfaction that you get when they do for you do without you asking.
It's the passion. The magic, the caring, the sharing.
The non-comparing. the being there when needed.
love is transparent.
It's a verb. It's something you external, its unique profoundly deep....
Love is more than a phrase. It takes off no days
Love will have you amazed. It's the greatest gift that was ever gave.
Love is selfless, not selfish nor Does love have a flesh
Or a race or a face. It's what we received when we inherited God's grace
Love will get you through a bad day or put a smile on a sad face
Love is great mixed with Everlasting faith, love will make you fast from hate
Love is the essence of existence love will lessen the resistance
Love is insisting on persisting through the oppositions love is giving
Love is listening, it's providing What's missing
Love is forgiving who has done you harm, all for Better Living.
Love have no senses, it's a spirit love doesn't have a price tool
Love is free ,Love is revival. Love starts right with you
Love will never fight you love is good to fight for
Love will help you right your wrongs. Love will get you through when those nights is long
Love is real love is an emotion.

Table of Contents

Cryonyx

Should I even care that you're not even here?
one of the biggest days of my life
you're not even there.
I haven't had the slightest clue
to begin to think that where?
Wherever you're at, which is weird and rude
I think back, matter of fact
I think that we're... Through
And I never wanna hear from you!
We're not compatible, it's not that I'm mad at you
But you can't make up the lost days
that I had with you,
You wasted my time and my energy
which cannot be replaced with.
With whatever you're giving me
I shiver at the bad memories
please forgive me for my brash delivery

But I have to ask you. Where?
Where the fuck was you at?
I called your phone 7 times
and you never called me back.

You couldn't have even send a reply text to me
I friend requested you, you couldn't even accept
me.

It's not that I can't live with the fact that you
rejected me,
I'm just mad at how you did it; it really
affected me.
Should I even have listened to your poor excuses?
When you love somebody, you don't ignore them
That's not how you do it.
Now I'm out here looking stupid...
spending valentine's day alone
in a drunken stupor…
because of cupid.
My hands bleeding from clutching this rose.
I was sooo foolish
To think that you would ever show up I knew it!
Another lame one to put in the excuses folder
I'm used to it. Now that I'm older,
I find that you were a much colder
and such a cobra.
Now I get it.
I was looking for love and a family,
and you weren't really with it
You ain't understanding me.
You could just spare me the bullshit
If you weren't with the commitments,
you could have saved me of my sanity
Instead of keeping me dependent,
On the false hope you were handing me.
You bitch!

I just really wished you woulda filled me in on
your decisions,
instead of me sitting in a prison
envisioning the life, we were to be living
You sold me a dream that now seems quite
ridiculous,
Come to think of it,
your lies were remarkably conspicuous
I'm such an idiot!!!
You could have sold me the Brooklyn bridge,
I was young, and strung, naive, deceived and
innocent
I really started to believe that it was all my fault.
Now I'm starting to see
how you patched up your deceits
with the stuff that you bought
You even kept the receipts
so that every time that we fought
You would make me feel at unease small,
appalled, stricken with remorse,
But it was me.... that helped you get on top of that
high horse.
I don't understand,
after a week, you got a new man,
and you were buying him a Porsche.
That shit was weak, But the blame was on me of
course

You started arguments to throw me off.
Just so you won't get caught
I never even cheated, well maybe I flirted.
Was that a good enough reason to throw away our purpose?
Was it worth it?
To throw our relationship in the furnace;
All that hard working I was really sincere and earnest
Or maybe I was an underservant of your love.
I'm uncertain
I held it down all year around,
played the clown in your circus.
I treated you like a queen,
but you treated me like a servant.
Had me like a fiend
not even a human being or a person
Do I deserve this?
all the downing and the curses
My head pounding,
I'm drowning in these currents
Maybe I shoulda been more observant
Because then I would have seen it coming
or at least I would have heard it.
And these tears wouldn't be on my face running.
you're like an onion, got me crying ...
your layers were pungent.

Or maybe I'm being punished,
for my past player ways or something.
I couldn't help it,
you had me going crazy and buggin'
You really had me gladly,
in love with you so madly
Now I'm left with this tragedy,
Professing my heart for you emphatically.
But what did u do? Made an ass out of me.
All my friends joked, poked and laughed at me.
My heart was torn apar
t and started to freeze gradually.
I gave you everything you wanted and needed.
What more can you ask of me?
But I'm glad that you are free,
Free now as we speak.
I can't get over the vindictiveness and bitterness;
the past was deplete.
Your passion was weak.
That which you displayed.
I should've been left when my heart was betrayed
But I guess, I was too afraid to step so I stayed.
To this day I'm still vexed,
I have nothing else to say.
I thought what we had was special but it ain't.
I think that it's best that you go
, and I'll go my way.
What I invested into you

has now all gone to waste.
I feel so disgraced, can't even show my face.

This whole healing process
has come closer to some sort of closure.
Just to be honest,
I don't think I would ever get over ya
We don't need a disclosure,
I would never exposure ya
And let everybody know what
kind of person you are.
To all your friends you seem to be perfect by far
you would never let 'em see the prices I paid
to purchase these scars.
I still keep your memoirs, your purses and bras.
Even though I feel worthless and small
It could've been worse after all.
You gave me a purpose and I saw it coming
before it happened.
But I was caught in the actions of your
satisfactions.

Shit happens!!!
for a reason. That wasn't an accident,
But now I'm bleeding.
That's what I get from living through my passions
Now I see it!!!
I wasn't paying attention to mad shit,

now I'm getting my ass kicked
Not to mention…all the backlashes.
Imagine, the lies I had to tell the guys.
To cover up and disguise,
I used shades to hide my eyes when I cried
Yes, I'm strange and deranged, but my heart died!
My soul was paralyzed…
If I ever did You wrong, 'forgive me' I
apologized
For the times I was dishonest.
And for whatever else I did to you
For you to make my heart to cry onyx.

Me n u

See what your love did to me.
Helped me create a new me.
Ooh wee I gotta love Jones.
Sushi on the plate not cake,
Your great like the late 2-3 wait.
The fire is in its place.
don't escape.
Let those Moscato grapes
percolate for the taste.
Let's chill and build.
have Conversations that's real
If you will, I'm thrilled,
I'm anticipating its surreal.
You give me something that I can feel,
without my hands.
A house can't be built
without a plan or on sand.
I understand, because I do the knowledge.
I do acknowledge what you do for me.
I'm astonished.
My flaws will be polished,
Let me tour your college,
So, I can learn you.
And get hooked on your phonics,
You will get your turn too
My crooked Ebonics
got you looking for houses.
Want to put my throne in your home
and make it our own… think about it.
Sweetheart, it's okay

**you can open up.
You ain't got to be afraid.
The best, I hope for the both of us.
I won't provoke or revoke your trust
Just don't croak or rust. We leveled up,
Here's a toast to us. We persevered.
No curses or fears
would ever impede our progression,
the worse is in the rear.
You're perfect dear...
At least in my eyes
We can watch the sunrise
On high tides
We're connected no Wi-Fi
My whole life,
I have searched for you.
Put in that work for you.
Thank God. I'm so merciful,**
You're my personal
**I don't want to share you.
Let you be the first to know
that nothing can compare to you.
I'm forever going to be loyal
because it wouldn't be fair to you
for me not to be.
I care and I'm here for you
I do solemnly swear to put you first,
to be there properly for better or for worse
and through severe economies.
We got something that's real,
it's more love than lust
plus, you can't spell prosperous**

without an US
In God we trust, and
till death do us apart.
I knew from the start,
That you would cuff my heart.
The way that you treat me,

the way that you feed me,
You would go through hell
with ice skis if need be.
That's why out of all the stars in the sky,
I chose to be with you,
You're more than qualified
Boo it's only me and you.
You're certified...in my heart you deserve to reside
And I ain't ashamed to say it.
You put some worth in my life.
I floss my affirmations
and affections I receive from you.
You're such an inspiration,
I still can't believe it's true
Me and you
makes my life feasible.
The only woman that I like
And ever need is you.

I love you so much,

Words can't even explain
what your hugs and your touch
do to my brain.
I never lose with you,
I always gain.
You helped me get through the loops
In my darkest days of pain.
That's why I gave you my name
And vow to stay faithful.
I promise I won't change,
And will love you every day, boo.

I wonder

Hey sweetheart can I talk to you for a minute?

I guarantee you'd be awesome when I'm finished.

My pictures had you blushing when you saw them.

I ain't rushing, I'm sincere and I mean this

you deserve love and affection.

I want to give you a new life, you're a blessing.

Your eyes have this hypnotic effect in them.

I promise I won't change once you accept this

You're beautiful on the outside and inside.

I know you're skeptical,

But you'll be glad that you tried.

How Passionately am I?

Of wanting love? I can taste it.

I have a sweet tooth and you're my favorite.

I know you have a lot going on, I 'll be patient.

They say good things in life

come to those who be waiting

My mind be in a Matrix, when I'm thinking about you

Let me caress and soothe,

And heal where you are bruised

Call on me, I'll be there in a few.

And if you ever get horny, I'll be there to enthuse.

Your ex should never sabotage your next.

Let me relieve your stress; put me to the test.

But I ain't going to force you or push those issues.

I just want to love you, hold you, and kiss you...

Ever since you gave me your number

I traded in my Summers

I'm ready to be your lover. baby you're a Wonder

Under... no circumstance, would I hurt you ma'am

Or dessert you, and, You're worth that chance

You have earnt that stamp...of a true Queen.

Your love is a drug and I'm a true fiend.

I'm addicted. I must admit it.You gave me a new meaning,

Every time I visit, I relived it. You're here for a reason

Our drives match. Our ambitions, intact

We have to keep our intentions and visions attached

to the goals we made... never thrown me shade.

Always show me love in so many ways

So many days, when I was lonely, you consoled me.

Always kept it real when we build never phony

ever since you told me... how you felt... I knelt

Because you told me you never wanted to be

with nobody else

I felt the same way, the same day

I proposed to you. what I'm supposed to do

I was close to you; my life, I owe it to you.

Without you, I wouldn't know what to do.

I'm cool, with spending the rest of my life with you.

I feel like this is the best and the right thing to do.

Elusive dreams

I can't change you,
so I mines well replace you
I ain't the type to fist fight or chase you
You so Disgraceful Let the next dude fuck face you I hate you
You let him cum on your frontals and give you facials
How you gonna front boo I made you
I Don't even have the courage to face you
I don't have nothing else to say to you
as my wifey I embraced you

Now I'm likely to erase you Out my life
you so ungrateful
You Can't even say thank you to the gifts I done gave you
New whips and appraisals
I uplifted and praised you
Made a way for you
And what you do I don't love you I hate you
The one ain't you
Wish I can Unpaint you
Mona Lisa ....you owe on my visa
Now I'm having these wet lucid dreams
you were too good as it seemed
Now I'm vexed past extreme
Pass that weed. I need that sativa
Barely believed ya
But I loved you so much ...I would see stuff...
And ignored it
wish I can take back all all of it
That's a fact fast forward it
But past is enormous
Now I'm on sick, wished woulda been called the quits
Now I feel like a dick in font of all my friends
Cause they all gonna say "see I told u"
Yeah whatever I'm anti-social
Use to post you On my Instagram and Facebook
I get it damm.. I'm lame I took
A hoe. And try to turn her into a house wife
Don't even sound right
I know down right
Stupid. I was SOOO foolish
Unwoke. Stroke by Cupid u stupid bitch

Forgive Me?

Incorrectlyapologetically

I'm sorry but that's all I can say
Please don't let that one-minute
mess up a good day.
I wish I could say and express the way I felt.
I thought you would stay
till I was in a better mental health
And sober,
I told ya I didn't want you to react off of the
emotions
that I had for you when you told me you were
going.
Now I'm mad and my heart is broken.
I won't do bad “too late” yeah, I know it.
But I was hoping,
You changed your mind and decided to keep me
company
I can understand that you weren't feeling
comfortable with me.
You didn't want nothing else to do with me
, I was pissed
Maybe we should have gone to the Ritz,
Then this would have not been a good date
that went wrong now I'm sick.
But I did get to shoot my shot, but I missed.
You dodged me, turned your face
when I went for a kiss
Honestly, it was probably me being a dick.

I ain't in the ordinary.
but you you're extraordinary.
You're flawless and Sweet smelling like a
strawberry treat
Fine, juicy like fruits off a vine. You are divine.
Whether you know it or not, or in due time.
You were confused and blind, ain't used to a guy.
Flawed, designed. Quite foolish was I
Thinking of you can be the ying to my yang,
the vision to my aim.
In addition to my game,
bad decisions were made.
Please just open up that heart to me.
Give a part to me, pardon my peeves, please.
Honestly. you're an honor to me.
A rare sight to see.You ignited me, and
enlightened me.

I'll erase those pains, embrace those reins.
I'll fight I will not cease.
You Stepped out of my dreams
I confess I'm a fiend.
I'm bugged you're a drug. I'm addicted to your
touch.
I'm just in need For your love, I'm hopeless
I hope this doesn't sound too obscene.
But I noticed you make me feel good,
so good I wanna shout and scream.

I want to be the man that you need, the man that helps you to succeed.
So please accept my apologies, baby that wasn't me;
I was intoxicated with your emotions and Jack D

do you still love me?

Crazy beautiful

You tell that me you're crazy, that's okay baby I get it.
I'm going to be your therapist and give you that prescription you've been missing.
You have one mouth and two ears for a reason.
You need to do more listening and be more obedient.
You hear, then I might be here for more than a season
and give you something to believe in.
And Stop trying and relying on experiments.
If you can see it, you can achieve it.
I can put you in a position to win again.
But you got to choose me like a spearmint,
and soak up these mental crucial nutrients.
And not be choosy like Suzy, who fear most men.
Then maybe we can stack bread and ideas like a pyramid.
Then things would take off from there,
and go smoothly like a blueberry nutriment
See miss What I can't do is all that weird shit
I know most dudes got you confused

and your tired of hearing it
don’t confuse me with them again
because I’m not him and him
With all seriousness,
you’re too beautiful to be smoking a cigarette.
Why are you single again? I’m curious.
You haven't been dating, just waiting furious
That a guy like me would come along
that you can relate with.
You're weary sis?
Have patience because life can get so delirious.
(chuckle)
But I ain’t playing.
Yeah, these cats out here are foul mad flagrant.
But I love your smile,
you drive me wild with your fragrance.
(Smell noise) no miss, that’s not loud, that’s frankincense.
But I ain’t a saint miss, I have my own issues
But I’ll make you famous. Come here, let me kiss you.
Your lips looking official, glowing like a crystal.
I’m grown, when we go out
you can pick anything on the menu.
You can have whatever you want,
that's just what men do.
And I’m not gonna front,
I really adore your mental.
You might be all that I want,
shall we continue?
We can hit up the Barclays or a Westside venue.
You got your guards up for what?
I'm just trying to defend you
You down on your hard luck.
I just want to amend you.

I wanna know all about you
and what you're in to.
How do you make your revenue not to offend you?
But I need to question you just like this is an
interview.
Then we can attend to Washington square park.
To be fair I wouldn't compare,
I just wanna share your heart.
Come here!
I know it's been broken in so many pieces.
And it's frozen. I just wanna hold you all weekend.
I'm not here to hurt you or desert you.
I just wanna accentuate the worth in you.
And want you to see it.
I know you got a curfew,
because you have to attend to your daughter.
Relax I'll have you back in a few,
until then let's blend in with the water.
Let our conversations flow like the Hudson.
I know men be buggin'
I already told you I ain't him. I'm a gem.
A king preparing to be some woman's husband.
I may look like I be thuggin'
but I'm done with them corners and the druggin'.
No longer do I be hustling, illegally.
Plus, I'm Muslim, I believe in *Hadiths*.
Not for nothing, you're looking kind of sweet.
I can tell by your teeth that you take care of yourself
plus, I hear it when you speak.
Your gear on fleek, you're not a thrill that's cheap.
And not the type to let your business
spill in the streets.
Be my peace, imma be your harmony.
The extra arm when you need
efficiently, not partially.

Pardon me, I got an old school swag.
Chivalry ain't dead,
I ain't like the other dudes you done had.
I will get you ahead,
make sure you don't misuse your bread.
Want to know if you know how to use your head
before I get you in the bed.
It's not all about the physical when I visit you.
It's more about the experiences
and visuals that I can give to you
Cause I need to know if your sane
before I entertain you in my living room,
give it room to grow,
you can't assume you know
all about a female.
You're gorgeous and all,
but I pay attention to the miniscule details.
So, before we go to the mall
talking about shopping,
I need to know if there's brains to match the beauty
because I got options.
Then after a few weeks we can talk about relationships
and where we taking this.
All that I ask is for
Is for you to be faithful miss
And not show up at my crib with all that craziness.
Your face and skin is flawless;
I have to admit.
But I need the whole package,
not just half of it.
You're crazy beautiful, you're crazy and you're
beautiful, And I'm Dr. Feel Good,
I'll make you feel good if you're suitable.

Merlmaid

I don't want that girl that's into pill popping,
'love n Hip-hopping and twerking.
I need someone who I can rub their feet after a hard day of working.
someone that has more than a generic purpose.
Someone that accepts me and my flaws,
knows I'm not perfect.
Someone I can learn
with who I could take turns with.
on dates like I pay for the meal,
she pays the waiter if they earn the tip.
I need someone who's not afraid to learn and sit
who can pay attention, get enriched,
then return the gift
each one, teach one, I just need one.
Even though I'm a guy,
I still get shy when I see her.
I don't know why or even her name.
Let's call her Gina;
She drives me insane.
Her smile can light up the whole Coliseum.
My heart was locked up,
she gave me a glimpse of freedom
her ex... sucks to be him
Because if I ever get the chance,
I'll show her romance in per diem
Abundantly, yes, she is something to see.
She is beautiful from the top of her head
to the bottom of the feet.
She's so sweet,
would get any non-diabetic addicted.
She's splendid,

I don't know where this is headed
, and I can't predict it.
This moment I live in,
it's bliss, unrestricted.
slid my business card on her windshield,
I hope she gets it.
She gives me chills,
I hope she calls me, I've been waiting patiently.
Her smile is so radiant;
her personality is veracious.
She's so amazing,
I anticipate for wonder woman to make her way in,
the gym,
she motivates me to do that extra rep,
I'm getting slim
, yeah nevertheless
I'm going to take that extra step on the treadmill.
When I see her, I'm like yes!!!
But I'm Dead still,

she's a real live gorgeous goddess in the flesh
But yet, she's still kind, courteous and gives
respect.
OMG.
I just know I'm not going to be that lucky...
but maybe
The way she smiled back at me got me blushy,
I know crazy.
It took me about five whole months just to say 'Hi'.
I ain't gonna front,
I liked her
ever since her graceness has hit my eyes
I was kind of surprised when she replied
to my card, I was like either she a social butterfly

or maybe I am really a lucky guy plus she's a Gemini
so, she can understand a cancer's struggles
we just wanna be loved and treated fairly and maybe cuddled. ☺
She instantly erased all my troubles and depression,
I know with her I can overcome any storm and there's a heaven
Her kind words were like a harmonic progressive medicine
And I told her 'I promise you'll never be second again.
I want to be more than your homie, lover, and friend.
I want us to be that love story that never ends.

But first I wanna get to know you.
I wanna know your desires
wanna know your hopes, fears
and plans when you retired.
Yeah, I know I'm weird,
but you get me higher than any drug supplier

I know you're working on yourself,
I don't want to impede that,
but you have something so pure and specia
l and I need that.
I just wanna be that someone you can talk to;
where you can find relief at
I wanna know your goals,
then motivate you to achieve that.
And I see that,
you're beautiful
so you probably attract all kinds of individuals.

I also see you're sensual
and a survivor from all the things you have been through
And you're a ten too,
so hopefully you can attend to
one of my poetry slams venues.
It's alright boo you hold my hands, I ain't gonna bite you
And I can see it on your face, yes, I'm excited too
I know you're not the type to move at a fast pace,
but I would like to prove
that there are still some good dudes out here,
make you laugh to lighten up the mood.
I wanna heal, wherever your bruised
your pain, I will like to soothe.
Hopefully soon, we can grab a bite...then spoon.
I mean by the river, walking and talking,
watching the moon
I wanna know all the bad things you been through,
so you won't have to go through it again
I never want to see you frown or looking down,
want to grant your every wish
I want to be your favorite dish;
I want to be your soulmate at 86
I want to be the one that you aged with,
you could even be some crazy chick.
Then I wanna be your *Xanax*, your *Thorazine*
and or your *Celexa*
I can't wait for the next opportunity to get next to ya.
I come with no extras,
no crazy baby momma drama
Just maybe a little insomnia
because I can't sleep without you.
I'm just being honest ma,

I don't want to breathe without you

I'm suffocating by the possibilities
of you really feeling me.
And contemplating on saying something
because the anticipation is killing me.
There's no ventilation for me to even speak
you got me weak
maybe next week I'll say it,
because I don't want you to think
that I'm playing
or I'm trying to move too fast
That I only have eyes for you,
damn I knew a good thing wouldn't last
She says she's not looking for a man
so, my invitation she passed
I understand her hesitations;
says she's been hurt by relationships in the past
and that she was only into dating,
exclusively nothing serious.
How delirious is that!
I asked her what the difference was,
then she hit me with the most finessed curve
Now when I message her, I get a 'do not disturb!!!!'
She got some nerves.
I forgot my words when I saw her in person
to ask her what was the disturbance.
But she told me that she would rather be lonely
because feelings only cause turbulence
And her hurt by men
will make her unable to be in love again,
and she doesn't want to further with this.
I get it, she just wanted to be independent
and probably was turned off by my persistence
And ever since this, things became awkward,

she sees me, but I don't even get a recognition.
She just wanted to be free like a mermaid in the sea,
and I wanted more of a commitment
I was talking about building a family,
and starting a business,
she went off and ended it
No hard feelings, we are still friends,
but I just can't date
without having a wife as my intentions.
And she can't relate,
so, she will just be another mermaid in the sea
swimming with the fishes

In-patient

You don't have to ignore me or not call me
you could've just told me you weren't beat
or was just bored of me
I get it. We're indifferent?
My personality is addictive, and you want to be independent.
But I wasn't even trying for a relationship,
You're the one who mentioned it.
I was just trying to get to know you,
why are you so defensive miss?
Those words in the poems I wrote; I meant them.
Maybe I was just too excited, guess I miss then?
Before I even got a chance to shoot my shot,
you choose to flop.
But my heart's still going to beat
whether it's bruised or not
It's a shame we really would have been good amigos.
I can tell your good peoples, but I know it's me though.
I get very enthusiastic like an addict
before they're about to take a hit
At least I know that good girls do exist
I do miss, hearing your voice,
seeing your smile though,
Why yooo! I got to be so sentimental,
I don't know.
I ain't gonna keep hitting you up,
I have seen you've had enough.

Got me on, do not disturb, sum nerve. I must suck
In making friendships with gorgeous women;
They all seem to think I want an instant relationship.
I hate this shit.
Part of it is because of my sign in zodiac,
Sensitive ass cancer
***sucker* for love but I can't control those facts.**
Plus, I was a crack baby, love is like *Coke* to me
I was hoping you see, I'm real and be open to me.
Not concealed, everything about my life can't be revealed.
I'm not perfect then, and would never will
If ever you feel like texting me
or getting next to me,
feel free,
your presence is like an extract fermented in *Pepsi*,
refreshing, oh this mess I'm in!
I'm impatient, a patient withdrawing from your medicine,
when the pain from the heart ache sets in.
And the realization that we are not going to make it,
I'm going to feel dead again.
When I needed you to talk too,
I guess you were too busy or bothered.
it's all good, I understand, no I'll wills we be harbored
I'm used to being abandoned and stranded,
I'm numb from it.

When I managed to show too much love people run from it
Now can put that energy on working on my stomach
I was over eating.
When I'm depressed, I tend to be emotionally distressed leading to me underachieving.
Maybe one day, you would see it,
I could have been your best friend or soulmate, but you wanted to be a mean bitch.
Not even given me a decent reason
or a common courtesy and tell me how you felt
You just ignored me and avoided me like I'm just somebody else.
I kept telling myself, not to get my feelings involved,
Because people just use you for whatever they want,
then leave you in the fog.
Then they hit you with a curve ball, faster than Kershaw,
I swear to God, nothing seems to last these days or work too long.
Where did she go? The question is redundant, I know
Probably far away from me
falling in love with an average Joe
Now there's a lump in my throat a bump in my road,
No return texts, no calls, no friend request, or nothing. Nope

She vanished, she panicked,
probably moved to another planet
Now I'm stranded, damaged,
probably because I'm cancerous,
I'm emotional, I'm moody, I'm clingy, I'm a nagger, I'm highly sexual.
I will cry baby, I'm crazy, I'm arrogant, I'm impulsive,
non-affectual
I guess, I will be single till my death or when I get out of respite
Or when I'm not desperate
for a love that I never seem to get.

Muraena Helena

What you won't do, another woman will.
There are too many fishes in the sea
to settle for an eel.
No miss! I'm not trying to pay your bills.
But I would like to get to know you
maybe we can chill.
No, you don't need a drink or a pill.
Our conversations will flow, and make you think
I'm just being real.
Use your intelligence, you can let down your shield.
I'm not like the other men
that you have met in this field
What he did is irrelevant,
I'm not here just for a thrill,
I want to build a fellowship,
not something that can easily fail;
Like a quick relationship
that can turn into nil
Or a *situationship*
that will have us at a standstill.
We can get to know each other
While I prepare you a meal.
But I ain't gonna smother you,
I'll be fair when we deal.
I have a romantic arsenal.
we can go out to the carnival
and ride the Ferris' wheel.
I want you to get to know me
and not how I appeal.

To be honest don't sink to the bottom.

Because there lies,
Lies, doubts, hopelessness
and shallow problems
Flaws, Yeah, got them.
I ain't perfect, I'm a person,
but I worship, and I'm solemn.
I think we met for a purpose
meaning I believe in investing
if you're worth it.
I want your love and affection,
not just your surface.
One day I want a wedding
and the clock to stop turning.
A love that is timeless
and honest like virgin.
But maybe you just don't get it,
or you don't understand.
Why would I ever agree
to share you want another man?
I would rather have you to myself
if that's selfish then I am
I want to provoke plans,
For us to evoke the sands of Brazil and chill…
Not to approach as dammmm…
Another argument!
It doesn't matter who started it.
Because we both end up heartless again.
Part is suspense.
but I still want to see where this goes.
Plus, I love seeing you

when you are wearing those, whoa!
Don't poke holes, let me do that.
Don't take your past relationships failures
out on the new cat. don't do that.
Give yourself a chance,
Be loyal and faithful,
Then return the romance,
Uncoil, then be grateful.
Give me both of your hands
and be all my options.
You could be in the cockpit,
just let me be your pilot.
I'll get us to the destination,
But first you have to ditch those reservations.
Trust in me, perfection needs no explanations.
I just want to be your all;
The only one that make you come and run to
when you need or call.
I ain't insecure maybe a little unsure.
Is this a 'friends-with-benefits'
or do you want more?
Are you trying to explore?
Or trying to build a kingdom?
I may not, or can't fulfill your income,
But I can fill your heart with love
and then some.
We got to start from the ground.
Then make our way on our feet.
Besides, Rome wasn't built in a day or a week.
I'm no Caesar, Senorita,
So, I don't need you to be a diva.

Just need you to be supportive
and be here when I need you.
I want us to want the same things
our names on each other's rings,
amongst other things.
And you, to be a mother to my seeds.
Genetically you might be better than me.
Because you look so beautiful f
rom your head to your feet.
Don't be extra with me.
Show me your devotion.
Show me that you're focused
To your coyness be my lotion.
If you can be the key my happiness
Then I would want you as my miss.
I'll shower you with a love that's so passionate.
I sit as I fish,
thinking of a love that's everlasting with bliss.
All I'm asking is this
Can you Keep it real with me?
And not be an ill to me?
There're too many fishes in the sea,
and only one me, can you fulfill my needs?
Caught in the reels, can you feel my speech.
I want you, to want me.
And not be just another eel in the sea.

Endless love

Forever and ever
you hold my heart treasures
I pray that we will never sever
I would always want to be together
I'm here for you
I care for you
This love I have inside
I will give it all to you
Nothing can compare to you
I swear it's the truth
My heart tells no lies
The day I looked in your eyes
I was hooked and by your side

Baby momma drama

Baby you keep telling me
I'm not the one for you repelling me
I ain't out here committing felonies
I'm trying to excel in these streets
Righteously
why you wanna fight with me
Acting feisty see
I ain't trying to be like them please......
I'm trying to ice them sleeves
That you wear.... got you a new pair
Of Masialagos
Dodging these pot holes
Doing thee impossible
to put pots on them stoves
I don't flock to them hoes

I'm just working to put food on the table
you are acting rude and unfaithful
I paid for your school
Our kids got good grades they improved
What u want me to do....
I'll pray for you
Make a way for you
Stay don't be cruel
My past precedes my present
They ain't trying to hire a felon
Plus, we mis leaded by our president
I lead and I represent the black seed
Please don't bash me, I'm trying
Every day another Blackman dying
They not justifying it they just denying it
Going to war on the same drugs they are
supplying
please........I just wanna see my seeds
Don't keep them from me
Because we couldn't be
What u wanted us to be
Wait...... don't leave
I'll pay the lease at least let me teach
My kids How to be a man and achieve
I understand your Grieve
We had plans that couldn't be reached
And demands that we couldn't keep
I'm a man and a G
But I'm talking to u candidly
When I call you, I expect you to answer me
I wear the pants, sheeesh
I ain't trying to argue or stalk you
I just wanna hold the peace
please can I talk to you

A blind man can easily see
The love I have for you and my seeds
At least you can be graceful and faithful
It's ok boo
I can't force you or make you
I ain't mad at chu
Just don't bring my son around passive dudes
I won't spazz at you That's all I ask of you
Don't have them calling another man "daddy"
Just because I don't do everything
that u asked of me
I take care of them
it's just that we don't see eye to eye
I don't mind giving you money,
I just don't wanna supply your highs
I got receipts I have to keep
Just so that child support
doesn't dock my pay every week
You keep threatening me and bashing me
On social media like I'm a deadbeat harassing
me
As we speak. you still won't link up to meet
Because you weren't involved in the shopping
sprees
It doesn't make sense to me
You wanted not to commit to me
you wanted your love life to be a mystery
I was out there working hard for us....
listen to me
I wanted us to have a family
All you had to do was assist me
I understand that we
wasn't gonna be perfect
But my mission was to please

Then for you to act so vindictively
Because I didn't want to be ya side piece
And abide to you getting high with khalif
I'm a man with pride and peace
In that house that you keep
I'm the one who supplied the heat
I'm the one who put dinner on the table
When it was time to eat
I guess you took it as me crying as weak
Nah I just wanted us to be a family
Without you lying and cheating
Why are you buying so frequent?
And out with a new guy every weekend
Maybe I'm gone off the deep end
But I sacrificed my life for you to be just a weak link
Now I need a drink
Just to drown these pains that I'm soaked in
Every time I think of my kids
having to grow up in a home that's broken
I never wanted this God knows this

I am trying my best to stay humble and focused
I guess I wasn't good enough for you to notice
My efforts my devotion
And just for the record I'm open
For us to one day be together I'm hoping
That you will finally get the message that I'm holding

Don't despise love

Hey sweetheart, you don't have to take things so
serious and precise.
I know Some decisions need incisions;
you may need a knife.
or a scalpel, to cut out those assholes
that's going to hold you back from achieving
the goals in your grasp boo,
just got to believe it, say it and mean it.
Watch out for those snakes that's in the grass too,
because they be creeping.
Do some meditation, set some plans then breath it.
Ditch the reservation,
it's in your hands if you can see it.
Nothing's gonna hold you back,
except the limitations in your mind.
That's a fact if you let it,
pessimism will control your time.
I want to put you in the position to regain
not mold your shine,
I'm different,
once you maintain and acknowledge this wisdom,
you will have a better understanding
to the college that I'm giving.
You just have to pay attention, that's your tuition
Retain the information, you do that by listening.

Be patient, your guide is your intuition;
it will provide you with answers in increments.
Yeah,

I may have more than a couple of screws missing
And I ain't the sharpest *karambit in* the kitchen,
But I'm sincere and I'm a man with a mission.
You're all about your fam and your religion
I get it,
I just want to hold your hands
and remove the divisions,
in your life. Then, add on with these inches.
Syke
I'm just playing, I'm only kidding.
As far as its your interests,
I'm interested in your submissions
on what it takes for you to be a better woman,
because life can be so viscous
Sweetheart, let me help you wash those dishes,
don't be so defensive.
I ain't gonna ditch you or be dismissive
when the trenches hit
I love a woman that's submissive,
and knows how to handle her businesses
And who's not afraid of commitments,
love, loyalty and honesty that's sufficient
My apologies for being a dick Miss,
and showing it, that was so inefficient
A penny with a hole in it, senseless,
I know, you want a man that's responsible and
attentive
, anything is possible,
I'm sorry boo about our past incidents.

But let me ask you this
not to harass you
but are you really over your past relationships?
If so, let's commence with this, get past them dudes.
Don't be scared to be committed again.
Stop binging on fast food, stressing
before you put yourself on an island like *Gilligan.*
Learn from those lessons;
you got to heal from within.
You shouldn't chill with friends, that's hoe-like.
That goes without saying.
If you are still in suspense,
let the good flowing out weigh them,
and we feel the thrills when we kiss.
I'm just saying this,
don't let the last man affect you
because you are special.
God sent angels to protect you,
no I didn't come here for your rescue.
But I may want to handcuff you, not arrest you.
And I won't stress you to even undress you.
Just to let you know, my intentions is more than
sexual,
I'm interested in conversations that's intellectual.

I'm stimulated and fascinated on a higher level,
so, let's take it slow
And not get too personal
but I want you as my personal
I don't wanna share or compare you,
you've been through the worse I know

I wanna converse with your soul,
we have both been burnt by the roads we chose,
but still, not chose to turn up our nose
A rose is still a rose as the Queen once said.
You can regain control because it's all in your head
You're still a flower,
never let a coward deflower you, in bed,
Let positive affirmations and situations
empower you instead.
And if I was you, I would get to know I.
You know why?
Besides, the way I come off and my flaws,
I really am a nice guy
Inside, I'm soft, but I just keep a hard shell.
Judging me by my looks, it would be hard to tell Every
book has a cover. I'm just being honest.
But once you discover what's inside the contents,
you would be filled with astonishment.
Of how I overcame deficient predicaments
with accomplishments,
Changed my bad ways, then admonished them
I went from having sad days and problems to *Zen*.
Would you acknowledge me then?

So, give yourself a chance,
don't give up on romance
My intentions aren't to hurt you,
I will let you know in advance.
I understand your circumstance;
you have been hurt by a man.
I will take care of you if you let me.
Anyway, here's my hand

Mr. thriller

You're a virgin in my eyes, because you never had Mr. thriller.
Yeah, its curved like a G, the G spot killer.
Every inch of that wet pussy I will fill up.
like envough imma give you something that u can fill uh.
Hold up, lay back relax.
Let that R Kelly 12 play play back.
Let you feel this thick cock. yeah, it's big and black.
While I'm kissing on you, baby can you dig that.
Cool...then move down to your neck.
Take my time get you nice and wet.
Sucking on your tits caressing and licking.
Prepare you for this unforgettable sticking.
Get u hot like a kitchen, access permitted.
Go down to your belly in a Z rhythm.
Lick between your thighs while you grind.
Get you high, in my eyes you're a dime.
Put your Thighs on my shoulders while I'm tasting it.
Bae you can rub my waves while my face is in it.
Tongue circle 8's like a nascar in slow mo.
Got the kitty purring. whoa whoa.
Give you that Mercedes treatments no more Volvos.
Let you cum.... rain on my parade.

Don't be afraid... honey you taste like lemonade.
Seems like you ready….
My dick is hard as algebra.
Extended like a 44 caliber.
As I look... into those sexy eyes mesmerized
but I really wanna see you spread those real legs wide
Put the head in, then take it back out.
Play with it then push it back south.
Ouch, ...u say. Sorry I will be gentle.
Then tear that pussy up like a rental.
After 8 strokes I'm going faster.
Let you know who's your master, then back up.
Flip you over. Hit you with that Mack truck.
From the back uhh.. then I fast fuck.
Pull ya hair choke, you until you gave up.
Shh be quiet, bite the pillow don't wake my neighbors.
Back shots phatty, bitch who's your daddy.
Then after... I want you to ride me like a cabby.
While I lay back feeling on your ass.
That pussy squeezing sliding in my shaft.
I feel you shaking vibrating from my drumming.
Hold up wait for me I'm coming

Permission

(With your permission)
I'mma put you in submission.
Switching numerous position
It's endless.
you cute and all sufficient.
beautiful. Delicious. let Daddy get it.

(With your permission)
Greenlight permitted.
Rub your body like physicians
give you what you missing
I'm vicious. Satisfy your interests
with inches ... tremendous

(With your permission)
imma Start out with slow kisses.
That Cîroc hitting
you got my cock on a mission.
Ocean scenic visions
cedar scented,
this hardwood got your sheets in drenches

(With your permission)
imma please you and lead you
to Orgasm. No spasms.
Pump back faster. I'm ya master
gag ya. give you these scriptures like a pastor if I have ta

(With your permission)
its spa back rubs.
Massages in the bath tub.
lozenges in the back of....(your throat)
faster. faster. grab the shower curtains
if you hurting. Ass up

(With your permission)
grasp ya.... Persian or Malaysians.
putting all 8 in, baby can take it
Put a smile on your face bitch.
This great dick.
Make you wanna taste it it's tasteless

(With your permission)
I'mma do all things. I said I would.
lay this wood like should. because I could.

(With your permission)
Imma stretch that pussy wide
Pressure applied
Put you out for the night.
Rub you down with ice
plunge you with this pipe........ this pipe

(With your permission)
Imma spread it.
you'll never forget this
Or regret it.
I'll cure your headaches if you let it,
yeah, I said it
This curve is magnetic
massively erected

(With your permission)
I'll let my blessings exceeds your
measurements
Don't be hesitant.
fuck you like the president
Trump in your tower
pump you in the shower
hour after hour

(With your permission)
Imma pound on you with power
baby powder fresh.
Yes, this the best yet.
Sour in the swisher
in the midst of Call me mister got your legs
pent up.

(With your permission)
imma give you all u needed...
knee deep in that sweetness
got you weakened
for the weekend
play that weeknd
we reeking.
sex and sweat yeah,
I'm beating yes

(With your permission)
imma make you feel this rapture
like Anita Baker.
see the way ya.
fiends for the tip like a waiter.
get ya weight up
we waking up the neighbors

(With your permission)
taking off that makeup
you are taking off today Hun
Make you succumb by the 8th one.
The way I made ya cum
you calling out the great one "oh my God"

Best for me

She wants the best for me.
I used to move recklessly1
Effortlessly, let's just see... If I could change
for disaster I seem to have the ultimate recipe
let's just see….
Hey drive, is constantly testing me.
She's fine. Her mind and time she invest in me
Our chemistry is ecstasy
. I'm grinning when she message me.
Our Communication is telepathy
Sex with me... is not in her subjective
No objection. this big D needs to be respected
A mental connection.
Lasts way longer than a physical affection
she's spiritually invested
History is a lesson gotta learn from your mistakes.
She said I got what it takes
and it's my turn to be great
I yearn for her faith that she got in me.
She's concerned not fake as these thotties.
See I need someone who can can be my motivation.
Go on dates with.
Someone down for me there's no debating
She ain't about Procrastination
She's knows what she wants
but at the same time, has the patience.
To wait for it to come naturally.
Friends first Foremost actually, goes to bat for me.

She got me wanting. to strive for perfection.
She keeps me on my toes with my goals
never second guessing them.
She's the queen she's the essence.
She puts in the efforts,
distribute foods spiritual or chefs it.
She brings out the best in me, yes indeed.
I was yet in need, for love, yes is he.
But I ain't ashamed she erased all my pain.
Made me wanna change my face was full of strain.
She motivated me procreated me
Helped me back on my feet,
when I was weak, she elevated me.
In one point in time I hated me.
I had excuses from a to z.
On why I should hustle and play these streets
She came to me as a fresh breath of air
Showed me she cared told me she would be there
Life ain't always fair.
She erased my hopelessness and fears
Opened her ears unbroken my mirrors
She boosted my confidence
She made all kinds of sense
My life was plagued with all counterfeits. ....

She's real!!!

Sonic marbles

You say that you love me,
but you don't you hate me
I'm so fucked up lately
I'm going... crazy...
I'm ugly come save me
love you, you hate me
don't trust baby....I fucked. .... stay please....
I won't lie. I apologize It wasn't mine.... don't cry
Tear drops from your eyes....I didn't mean.... I
was so high
I was so mean I don't know why
Don't leave. Don't go bye
I was a fool I was so rude
I did things that I don't do
Can I show you, gotta lot to prove?

I owe you. I'm not that dude
Won't control you. No, I will not do
Wanna hold you soon as possible
I'll do what I'm supposed to do
I knew what I told you
I threw up all that soul food,
that you fed me I was so cruel
Stay please. My baby I hate me Don't erase me
Don't make me. Go crazy
Don't replace me. No wait. See....
I changed my ways I change my life
No more rainy days no more rainy nights
I'll make it right I'll make you my wife
I'll take advice. Just stay in my life
You the one .... you always was.
I was so young. I was bugged
I'm so in love I'll go nuts
If you opened up. For someone else
Our love. Trust. I fucked up
Can't take it back gotta make it back
I lucked up ... can't fake the facts
In love with her. No replacing that
I'm so sorry won't do it again
You are a part of me we're more than friends
More than a lover yeah to the end
I'll never hurt you ......ever again
Please forgive me I been on empty
I plead on my knees... for your sympathy
I grieved your memories do remember me
I need your energy I fiends for that inner peace
Baby don't go, baby don't go

I need your loving baby please don't go

Cold

If I rule the world, and I knew a girl
that shared same values,
We can clam up and remove the Pearl
It would just be...me and her
I would accentuate
What I see in her. Yes sir!!
She's the queen of my dreams... yes, her.
She completes me completely!!!
God, she sees in me
She loves me vehemently
She is easily the keys; the lock to my heart.
I'm not gonna start on how I feel...
Just stop!!! Chill.
She' real... In a world that's fake.
She's the icing to my cake.
My wife is just so great
A happy wife is a happy life.
But she won't sleep half the night
If I ain't acting right.
She's the queen...She cooks and clean.
In those books, she feeds the seeds.
It's not all about looks or green.
You can't buy real love, only imitation...
She got the strength of a nation;
She's tremendously patient.
But she won't be waiting
for me to get my act together
if I keep messing up, it would be a wrap forever...

She's my treasure, no ruler that can measure her.
There's no need for me to cheat and bring all that extra stuff
She only comes once in a lifetime she's my life-line,
To my seeds, take heed...
imma wife mines...When I find her,
This a reminder.
You better take care of that woman before your time's up.
And someone else slides up...
showing more care and concern you'll lose your mind *bruh...*
So, give her flowers while she's living.
Show her she special...
Give her kisses with emphasis...
Don't wait... until she goes,
Before you try to show
her that you love her.
She's just going to close her heart
because that's what you chose.
You rather hang with the Bros
instead of claiming her like gold
It's cold,
This world… that we live in
That's why when you find her
You got to value that woman.
If I knew the ending
from the beginning,
I would have changed my ways,
I would have done things differently.

But now I'll probably not get the chance
to show her romance,
Give her PDA (public display of attention)
and hold her Hands in public
She has seen me as great.
I didn't pay attention,
Now I'm paying the consequences
It happened in a sequence,
She was fed up,
Listening to keep Ya head up (r.i.p. Tupac)
…I never peeped it
Her heart...💔
I broke into pieces.
I was too busy being unfocused and conceited,
that I didn't see shit.
She's gone, Now I'm seasick.
Feeling like a penis, with thoughts of slicing each
wrist
She vanished,
Now I'm famished.
I thought we would be family,
that was how I planned it
But somehow, I managed to damage
What we worked hard for,
For a damn bitch.... Damn it!
I can't blame her,
I didn't use my brain *bruh*,
I was thinking with my other head
You'll lose, in that game of love
The pain that comes from heartbreak is unbearable,

embarrassing and unravishing
just terrible, I bare my soul,
But that's not going to help me.
I was so, helplessly selfish indeed.
I didn't take heed
to give her what she needs.
That love and affection,
Now I'm on bended knees,
begging please...
Like baby please, don't do this to me.
But I did this to myself, please don't leave.
She been gone,
I just never acknowledged it.
My heart won't allow it,
My pride can't swallow it
I'll vow to give anything,
Just to turn back the hands of time.
As a man I'm dying... On the inside
without my rider by my side,
I took a t.h.o.t. to where I reside.
I took *wifey* for granted,
Somehow, I thought she would remain standing,
Now I'm feeling maimed and abandoned.
Now... I'm with the 'should of's' and 'could 'of s'
With my shit she had to put up
I ruined that good love

Hood... gloves...357 snub

Without her,
I'd rather be in a tub full of blood.

Queen of Essence

I think she is worth it; she's so perfect.
To tell you the truth,
I don't even know how I deserve this.
Her body is something that any man would worship.
But I'm godly,
So, I got to let her put the work in to earn this.
She does Pilates.
She's mentally disciplined plus she learns quickly.
She's got a good head on her shoulders,
Queen Shikha invisible golden turban.
She's holding more just an ass,
she's got class, she's a virgin.
Because whatever past she has had,
I'm not too concerned with.
As long as she's here and sincere,
shows loyalty and she's earnest.
I don't care
and won't compare her to another person.
When I'm with her, nothing seems to be unfair or too urgent.
She's rare, nowhere on earth
you will be able to search and find this version.
Not even in Armenia, an encyclopedia or a cleric,
Could spell the words what I feel, she's so real,
in *cursive*.
She's so pure, I see greatness.

She's non-high maintenance, to fakeness, I'm allergic!
She tastes sweeter than a tasty cake mix,
but she's not for purchase.
You can't try to buy her;
money isn't her objective or her purpose.
Either she's going to school or with her family or she's working.
She's not into social media,
don't keep a remote in her hand consistently turning.
From one ratchet TV show to the next,
or wearing a skimpy dress because she's learning
about economics and politics
and not to accept anything less than a Birkin.
For her time,
Her mind is designed not to be in coercion.
See likes me for who I am
I'm nice and sweet and I'm assertive.
Her bad habits I burnt them
she adheres to the knowledge I instill
but I'm still nervous.
I get butterflies when I look into her eyes;
she will make onion cry…curtains.
"I don't want to be a player no more"
Pun intended, no more lurking.
She's a dream come true,
and whenever she comes through,
I'm thirsting.
She gives me that *Sprite* without codeine or preservatives.
Like *Napoleon*, I'll burn the bridge.

There’s no turning back to negativity,
she’s permanent.
My soul aches at the thought of her leaving me.
I would burn within.
That's why I do right by her, make a wife out of her
and stay affirmative.
I love to see her smile, she's so wow!!!
A perfect 10.
I give her the utmost respect and remain a loyal
gentleman.
I work hard all week to put her in a suite or a
tenement.
She swept me off my feet,
she’s so sweet like an Entenmann's.
She's royal a Queen, a gem,
a diamond in the rough. Then again
I am not trying to give her up
so, I would never violate her love.
I win I win!!!
I ain't afraid to display my affections,
she’s the queen of my essence.
And when she's in my presence,
she is my blessings.

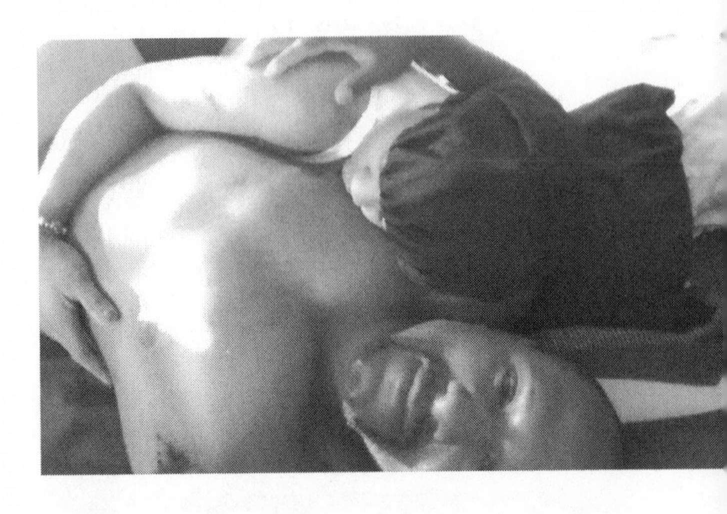

TGIF on a thirsty I meanThursday

Only if you knew how beautiful and suitable
you are to me guess we'll see what the future
holds
you should know I would never hurt you or
desert you
I want to learn you I can see the worth in you
Patience is virtual
I waited through a curse for you
if you're real I'll walk to the end of the Earth
for you
Seen you on that Facebook looking like a
straight crook
stole my attention with your face and looks
I know you wanted to see me live on VC
like this nigga's handsome, is it really, he?
Then when I heard your voice

I made the choice yeah,
I'm going to give it one more chance at Romance
You intelligent...
your goals and dreams are relevant
to what I was looking for
you might be heaven sent
I couldn't pass up the opportunity
after one conversation
I can see you and me in unity
your mad sweet, petite make any man weak
Freak in the streets
and lady in the streets
I swear that nothing could compare
to the feelings I felt
when your words hit my ear
TGIF..... but it was only Thursday
I thank God anyway her voice amazes
Good things come to those who wait
put away that steak
put these fruits and seeds on your plate
we didn't meet buy no accident
I see you I want you I go after it
We both asked for this....
busted our ass for this
Now I found you I want you as my miss
as my chick. Maybe
If you understand, we can travel
grip my hand walk the sands build a castle
out of gravel
Get the scalpel cut off all your exes
let them see the exit let em see us flexing

Tell me your confessions tell me your fears
Tell me your hopes and dreams
tell me you going to be here
Tell me that you loyal tell me that you Faithful
Tell me that if shit ever hits his fan that you'll stay too
Loyalty is a staple give me that I will stay with you
spend all my days with you baby boo
Maybe you,
are here for a reason or here for a Season
I don't know but your here and your breathing
Those spots I could reach it those locks I can key it
it's possible to achieve it with u on my team miss

Angel eyes

Hey, I know you have been hurt and deserted a lot
But it's going to be okay.
I can see your worth in your stock.
Even though times is grey, keep working, don't stop.
In your eyes, I can see the earth and the crops.
You have a purpose and you're not
worthless, you need to stop.
Thinking negative
because you earned your spot,
baby live,
get focused and return to that Gwap
And notice that you're here for a reason,
you wouldn't be here if you were not.
Even though you don't see it, you will rise to the top.
Things ain't always at your convenience,

so live life like the lox.
Off your experiences, have faith in yourself.
God will provide a way.
Those dark nights alone
will end up on the brightest day
Hey
you don't need a man; you need a plan
that alleviates you.
Someone will come through
that can really appreciate you.
Have confidence.
I know some men are only looking for the obvious.
But you got a lot more to give
than some cookies, be positive.
You're beautiful and suitable as a *wifey*, miss
and I see you get to that check.
you be on your *Nike* shit.
So, keep striving
even though the roads seem to be the rockiest.
you will reach them goals.
don't close up, you will block them gifts.
Persistence will overcome resistance.
I see you in the gym getting fit on your rocky shit
and you can tell your real ones
from the counterfeit
frenemies pretend to be there.
but u can't count on them when you're sick
or in a messed-up predicament.
I know it's ridiculous

but you're a survivor.
Everybody pays the piper; karma is a bitch.
But success is the best revenge
yes it can get intensive.
I see hope in your eyes.
don't despise or get defensive
all guys are not the same.
and the price you pay for pain can get expensive.
I get it. you win some. you lose some.
but you can't become incomprehensive
to love.
because we all need companionship.
I am not that man or him.
I just want to shower you with romance and gifts.
hold your hands and sit
at Central park and get into your heart
and into your mind
because to me you're a star
that just allowed someone dim your shine.
In due time. I will show you better than I can tell you
and all your exes are going to be sick.
admitted them to *Bellevue*.
Every time that I smell you.
the scent of your perfume brings me to my senses
and when I look into your eyes. I'm compelled to
get stuck in a daze like I have nothing to say
because I don't want to fail you.
I want to unveil you.
take away some of that weight off that scale too.

You have too much on your shoulders,
I just wanna to hold ya when you're available
I know you have a busy schedule;
I don't want to mess with you when you are at your occupation.
I know you work hard; I just want to be your compensation.
Give you stimulating conversations,
I may seem like I'm getting impatient
Because I don't like waiting
like I'm some waitress at *Applebee's*
But I want to see you happily and achieve
even if it's not with me
It will be, if it was meant to be,
I want to give you good memories
I want to make you smile every day of the week,
not just from 10 to 3
Like a part timer, it was hard to find you,
So I won't mess it up
Trying to be Russian,
I'm half black, half Arab. I'm tough as a button
For love I'm a glutton,
but sometimes it can become a punishment
I hope we can have fun with this
and see where it goes and run with it
You never know what can happen or what can become of this.

Wonder woman

She's always there for me keep an ear for me
Every time we speak, I'm not impaired I'm intrigued
Such a kind-hearted woman sincere and sweet
Really makes a difference
no matter where in the week
Every day is a resemblance
she gives me that significant
way of letting me know I'm a greater man
And I remembered it
I appreciate you and everything that you do
Ever since I met you my dreams have come true
You always come through
no matter what arguments we have had
You never really got that mad to just up and leave

no never did me like that
In my darkest times
you were like a sparkle of sunshine
And Sometimes I don't even know why
you even cared, I was barely there
I don't know if I deserved you or earned you
I know I'm hard to deal with
But your always concerned too

went through the extra measures
just to make sure I was okay
you made my pains go away
Soothe me, comforted me and confronted me
when I was doing wrong,
you wanted to best for me
Even when I was losing my charm
and went into a depression
it was never a 2nd guessing
on if you were gonna ride or not,
you rode with no efforts
I know everyone depends on you
to be that Wonder Woman
that you have become accustomed to be
Never even slacked
even though you got back lashed
for fucking with me
It must be something you see
that I can't see in myself
For you to be there when no one else
wanted to help
They Vanished in thin air and didn't care
But you never left me in despair
you leant me your ears
Even through the long distance

and the inconsistency's
Never would to leave me
in the cold with a thin sweater
You knew u would get better
that's why you never let up
This letter I wrote Blood as my ink
you gave me another reason to think
When I was locked up unreasonably in the clink
even when things weren't feasible
you help me see that a positive outcome can be achievable
I never believed in goals
I was just hustling blindly
just to see where it goes
Only led me to being confined
and the time just never froze
Those roads I chose
always ended up in the same place
a fate that I couldn't escaped
until I had to look at my own face.
and face life on its terms,
I rose Like a rose out of the cracks of the concrete
Even though I may seem to act nonchalantly
I'm very thankful for the kind gestures
And the mindful lectures that u bestowed upon me
You knew I was Innocent
regardless of those false charges thrown on me
Never disowned me or cloned me
Because a replicant couldn't represent

my wisdom and handsomeness is what you told me

I was so deep. Into negativity
you helped me see a better me
Even though your husband was buggin
thinking it was something that it wasn't'
you still wouldn't budge then
Because friends is a ship that doesn't sink
And you have shield me from this cold world
with a dozen minks
It wasn't cheap.
The price we had to pay
for our bond to stay was a leap
Of faith and courage
You knew I would flourish,
and I probably don't deserve this
But thanks for being there for me
when my own peoples couldn't be there when
I grieved
Or wouldn't come near me
You gave me purpose

Close to meet

I can't sleep because I'm tossing and turning
Yearning to meet, my soul is burning
It's certain that I like you, to my life I invite you
I know I'm ecstatic, I hope you're excited too
Never met no one like you so nice and cool
Sexy at the same time and believe in Christ too
There is no pressure, I want this to last forever
You're like the most beautiful hidden treasure.
I want this to happen organically and naturally
In fact, you'll see, that I'm the man that you need
All this seem to happen magically
Meanwhile you might be attracted to me
But what I really need is your heart to be attached to me,
And your mind to be aligned if this happens to be.
Yes, I'm the same guy on the phone;
The one who kept you company on your nights alone
I may not be a CEO yet... Nor do I own a corvette
But I can make your dreams come true that was far fetched
I like our chemistry, maybe it was meant to be
There's only one way to find out... on Christmas Eve
I want your presence as my present
Don't be reluctant or hesitant to accept this miss
It's evident… your doubts are irrelevant
because this was heaven sent, see the evidence

Ever since we started talking,
I felt us sparking.
I Can't wait for our souls to be paralleled,
no parking.
We got to see.... we got to meet.
I hope that you're satisfied with every part of me
I lose a lot of sleep, wondering where this can
lead
I'm willing to go the extra measures
just to see what this can be
Let me show you that I'm the one that you need
Manifest what I told you, the facts you can see
happily, ever after, let's start this new chapter,
let's meet
So, we can put into fruition of what we speak
Our conversations be so unique and deep.
Jonesing on the phone till we both fall asleep
Got butterflies in my stomach, filled with
anticipation
It's been a long time in the making,
I don't mind having patience.
My heart's been vacant
waiting for you to just to take it,
Can't wait to see that smile on your face and
embrace it…
It's been a while, but it feels so brazenly amazing
The clock is on the countdown, I'm so crazy
anxious,
I might just faint miss, I'm playing,
I'm saying.
Haven't felt this way since

Christmas eve, when I was a kid
and I was staying at my momma's crib
that’s how this is.
I’m impatient,

Pacing, facing, insecurities and inferiorities,
I can’t take it.
But that's just my conscience
I have so much confidence
because this love’s so pure.
I’m so sure, isn't it obvious?
My gut never lied to my face,
just be honest,
this makes me feel so hopeful
to know such a dope soul.
The way we connect through the internet and
telephone
conversations related with invigorating elations,
Calculating
how we are going to fit us in the equations,
Listening to the quiet storms until the day ends.
Thinking about you and how the time came and
went
Can’t wait to see you, so tired of these previews,
Every time my phone rings, wishing it would be
you
Kissing you in my daydreams,
thinking about how I will feed you
I need you, I breath you I can't wait to see you.

Y

Why is not answer baby it's a question

Maybe you don't know me
maybe you are second-guessing
I see your florescence
I'm Impressed by your freshness
Let's just undress this sundress miss
Suggestions suggestions
Nothing left with them exes
I see your angles and reflections
you ain't gotta change ya complexions
Mami .... Let me fertilize your soil
I'm stern but wise.... I'll spoil you
Come here and let me adore you
Explore you, I wanna see more if you
I wanna go on tour with you
Why? Because you make my heart beat
You make my soul woke here's my car keys
I was so broke not financially but spiritually
You deposited your love in my main artery
Your day starts with me not Folgers
Every time I hold ya I just wanna get closer
And closer never wanna let go of ya
You know what, I really do like you
To my life I invite you, you can meet my family

I'm the man you need can't you see
I totally recalled the day I met you
That day was special, it's marked on calendar
You pulled up in red challenger I just had to follow ya
To get your name and number I even made you smile
Took you to Mr. chows on the first date
You remember now?
Next week marks our anniversary
We went through mad adversities
At first it was me,
I was smothering you like pork chops and collard greens
Because I never wanted to see you leave
Personally, I was out of your league
I couldn't find work for weeks
I knew you wouldn't acknowledge me
if I told you the truth honesty my apologies
I just didn't want you to judge me
based on my time of need
and I see that God had blessed you with no allergies
and my life was screwed up,
technically I needed an Allen key
Because my whole life was hexed,
See That fact that I have narcolepsy
and I'm addicted to Pepsi
because of the fizz, caffeine and taste
Puts me in a bad space

Why? I don't know it's just is
And you ignoring my texts again
doesn't do it any justice
I was raised that women aren't to be trusted
But somehow you found a way
to bust that myth
I must suck at this
Because I'm quick to fall in love or lust
Because I love that shit
Makes me feel alive inside
gives me a false sense of pride
I remember nights
we use to Jones on the phone
Til the Am
until I'm arriving at work late again
I use to hate them alerts you use to get
I was so impatient
even though we just met I didn't say it...
But I wanted to wife you ever
since I laid my eyes on you
You were surprised I knew everything you
told me
I was hypnotized by you.
Why?
That's something I can't seem to answer
Maybe because imma cancer
And you're a Scorpio so I completely
understand ya
We both water signs even though I'm
borderline Leo

I will still romance ya
just don't lie to me though
my intuition is usually on point like a cactus
above average so don't join my fan club
Because I would never give a 2nd chance at love
Once you cross me you lost me
and my relationships Tend to end awfully
because you would never see no more of me
Just like that (snaps) in a blink of the eye
I can tell you bye and move on with my life
and won't lose no sleep at night

Why? That's just how it goes, who knows
When the hublots is gonna stop ticking
I can't waste time on some who is indifferent to my spirit
because in one instant we can disappear quick
I'm so glad that doesn't apply to you
Why you? Because you gave my heart a revival
My love was recycled
I don't have no problems letting the world hear my poem recitals
about you because I like you
Why? That's a good question you got
But I can't seem to answer it

But why not

Pain in my eyes

Dear mom you abandoned me,
stranded me
my whole childhood miss handled me
I ended up in the hands of he
or in the hands of she
had to go to grams for weeks
You chose a man over me
Disappointed me, we have plans to
meet
I'm damaged meat
Panhandled in the streets
for something to eat
my stomach was weak
you were running the streets
When needed something on my feet.
you walked out hustling for a
piece
Shuffling in the streets
fucking up my peace
Funking up my sneaks
scuffing up my cleats
try to play sports
but it was for your love I compete
But I guess I wasn't that important
As those other dads calling

shoulda left my bad ass in the
orphanages
If you wanted to get high
wanted to get fly
chasing all these guys
whose, chasing another high
Maybe you were right.
I wasn't worth your attention
I only got in the way of you
and your addiction
Every year.... another sibling
Another addiction to the benefits
and the food stamps we were getting
While you were out there drugging
looking for another husband
we were at home alone
with our stomachs grumbling
Wondering, when your gonna come
again
Then some men,
took me out our house
and put me in a village
That Started my nomadic pillage
I have no feelings
for another human being
you being the reason

Now how I'm supposed to live this out
when the one gave me,
life abandoned me
shoulda spitted me out
Or aborted me....
cuz you distorted me
now I can't completely trust a woman accordingly
Your love
That was what was important to me
You fed me bad milk, was how you spoiled me
And they say the apple doesn't fall far from the tree
all I ever wanted from you, was you to be a part of me
you took my heart out of me
and replaced it with anger
put me in danger, to be raised by strangers
I ain't gonna cry but I ain't gonna lie

you really messed up my life, putting pain in my eyes

Sucker 4 love

You say they look at you for sex
But I know you have way more to offer than your flesh
I want to see if we could really connect
Yes, you are fine, but I want to Get into your mind and entwine into your intellect
My main objective
isn't to get into your bed yet
But I do like your smile your style and profile
and the way that you wear your specs
Yes, with all due respect
I don't care about them other dudes you have met
Because you haven't seen nothing yet
It ain't fair to me, so don't compare me to your ex
I'm a rarity I might just be your best
I confess I'm not perfect
I come drama free
And I ain't gotta mislead you
But honestly....
we ain't gonna need to get too in dept
Let's have a conversation with mental stimulation
I suggest
But you gotta get passed your past and accept
This for what this really is let's start afresh
And see if our hearts could Kinect and mesh
Breath....

I want you live out your dreams t
hat seem far fetched
Give me a kiss .... "Not yet"
I was just playing baby,
maybe that was just a test
I just wanted to see how far I would get
Yes, I know you felt that hard,
stretched through the sweats
But it's not all about that nevertheless
I wanna see where your minds is at
before we flex
Because that broom will u get swept
of your feet
Then you'll be all confused Lost and weak
Talk is cheap....
so imma pay attention to your actions
See if this can be more than a physical attraction
imma be at this boutique
on 125th street and Madison
Then....... we can proceed to the Radisson
Shhhh before you speak here's my name
So won't have to ask again
And my tribe is Mandingo I'm an African
Only good vibes and lingo love to keep u
laughing miss
I can tell you ain't from around here
I peeped your accent and scents
Yeah, I confuse you and amuse you then act as if
I just want to do what we do then play neutral,
with my passiveness

then act like I never knew you,
once I get that ass, I split
off to the next muse,
trying to bend her like a pretzel
I fast as shit
I'm just a walking contradiction
but you give in to your addictions
Thinking your gonna benefit off my riches,
you must be having a sickness
You should have listened, to laurin hill
instead of being amazed by foreign wheels
Poppin pills, shopping for deals getting implants
then ducking the hospital bills
Then you woulda seen me coming,
a wolf in sheep clothes
Or heard the whispers Olivia,
wouldn't have been turned out like a cheap hoe
But your still oblivious, stuck in your ways,
amazed by what you see in your phone
And I must admit it that
I'm addicted to your kind in a sense
I'm always alone
A King with no throne, my house is not a home,
I'm always on the road
Looking for the next victim, someone innocent
to fall for my charm and wits
So, I can make them fall in love with me
and fill my abyss
But that pit seems to be bottomless
I have problem with this

Maybe because I grew up fatherless
and my mom was outside copping hits
I just wanna be loved in the way I was missed
something in my heart was amiss
That was my only wish on my Christmas list
that I never got to get
I still struggle with that, I know it seems to be
quite bugged
I tried to find it in drugs
but in that process, I turned into a slug
My friends talked about me,
drug my name in the mud
They Always did without me
, meanwhile all I needed was a hug
Ever since I was a child, I always been a

sucker 4 love

The end

About the author

Jaron Burnett, also known as Coolgmack is a freelance poet, rapper. who grew up in various cities of Westchester, New York? Raised in group homes jails and institutions, succumbed to the dark streets of NYC.

He spent most of his life in jails, chose poetry as a way out of the chaotic street life and made a vow to change his life for good while doing an unjustified long prison sentence. Jaron finds poetry as a way of communicating what is on his mind and hopes to change his society with it, showing them that there is more to life than circumstances.

He has performed in various open mics including Nuyorican Poets Café. He has various social media including YouTube, Facebook and SoundCloud Instagram all under coolgmack

Made in the USA
Middletown, DE
17 February 2019